A Volcano Adventure

Paul Humphrey and Helena Ramsay

Illustrated by
Jeremy Gower and Pamela Goodchild

CONTENTS

Evans

What are volcanoes and how are they made? What happens when they erupt? These are the questions we will answer as we take an exciting journey around the volcanoes of the world.

I didn't know there were so many volcanoes!

4

There are thousands of volcanoes in the world.
Over five hundred of
them are still **live**.

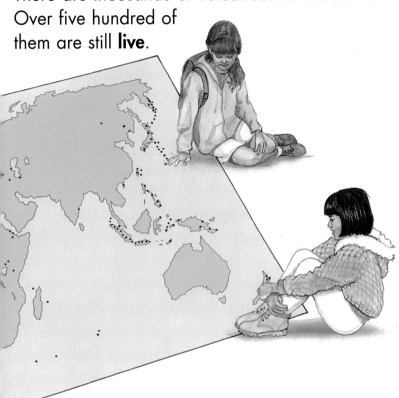

We start our volcano adventure in the Hawaiian
islands of the Pacific Ocean, where some of the
most active volcanoes in the world are bubbling
and fuming.

5

Here is the volcanic island of Kauai, one of the Hawaiian Islands.

Kauai

Oahu

Molokai

Maui

Pacific Ocean

Hawaii

The mountain peaks you can see are the tops of volcanoes.

Did you know that the island of Hawaii itself is the top of a volcanic mountain that rises 9,150 metres above the sea bed?

6

This is a volcano erupting on the island of Hawaii.

It looks as if it's on fire!

Inside a volcano the rock is so hot that it is liquid! That river of flame flowing down the hillside is actually molten, or melted, rock, called **lava**.

A volcano is an opening in the Earth's surface through which lava, together with pieces of rock and hot gases, bursts out or 'erupts'. To find out why volcanoes erupt, we must first see how the Earth is made.

Imagine that you could cut a slice out of the Earth with a giant knife. This is what it would look like inside.

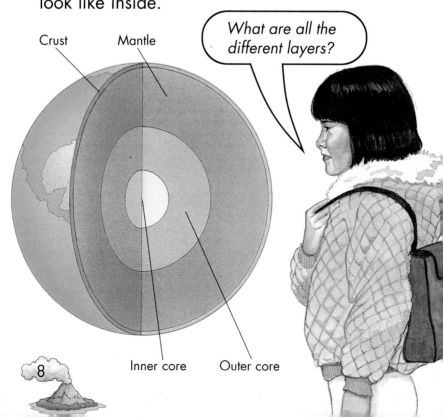

Crust Mantle

What are all the different layers?

Inner core   Outer core

The top, hard layer of rock that we stand on is called the Earth's crust. Deep beneath it is the **mantle**, a layer of hot, soft rock. In some places, this rock has melted to form **magma**. The outer core is made up of hot, liquid metal and the inner core of solid metal.

If you were to drill deep enough through the Earth's crust anywhere in the world you might find magma. You might even find it right under your own house!

Volcanoes occur where there is a weakness in the Earth's crust. Where the crust is weak, magma can force its way right up to the surface.

9

The Earth's crust is made up like a jigsaw puzzle
of massive sheets of rock called plates. The largest
of these are thousands of kilometres wide. The
plates float like rafts on the mantle below.

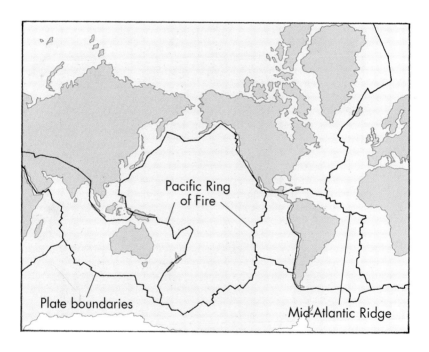

Pacific Ring
of Fire

Plate boundaries

Mid-Atlantic Ridge

Most volcanoes are found along the edges of
these plates, where the plates are either pushing
together or pulling apart.

Sometimes two plates collide, and one is forced under the other. As the plate sinks, the edge of it melts and becomes magma. The magma rises to the surface to form a volcano. This is how the ring of volcanoes called the **Pacific Ring of Fire** was created.

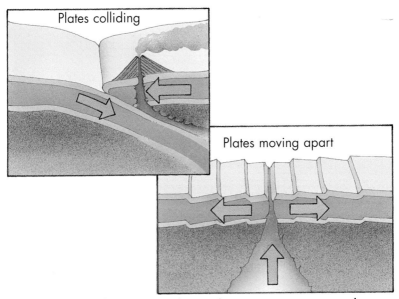

Plates colliding

Plates moving apart

Sometimes plates crack and move apart, and magma from below moves up between them. This is how the mountains of the **Mid-Atlantic Ridge** were formed under the Atlantic Ocean.

11

Now let's go and see what happens when a volcano erupts.

Africa

Nyiragongo

This is Nyiragongo in Zaire, Central Africa. Look at the boiling lava spouting out of the top of it.

This is what the erupting volcano looks like inside. The heat inside the **magma chamber** pushes the magma up through the **main vent** and out on to the surface of the Earth as lava.

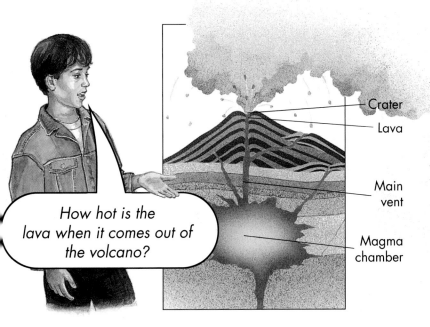

Crater

Lava

Main vent

Magma chamber

How hot is the lava when it comes out of the volcano?

When the lava shoots out of the volcano it is very hot. It can be over 1,250°C. Can you imagine how hot that is? The oven in your kitchen can probably only heat up to 250°C.

Volcanoes begin as cracks in the Earth, but with each eruption the ash and lava build up to create a volcanic hill called a cone.

Some cones are almost flat, like Mauna Loa in Hawaii (above). Others are tall and pointed, like Mount Fuji in Japan (opposite). The shape depends on whether the lava was thin and runny or thick and sticky when it came out of the volcano.

14

Which volcano was made from thick lava and which from thin lava?

Mount Fuji was made from thick lava and Mauna Loa was made from thinner lava. Thick lava piles up as it cools to form tall volcanoes, called composite volcanoes. Thin, runny lava spreads out into wide, flat volcanoes, called shield volcanoes.

Mexico

Paricutín

Some volcanoes are built up over hundreds of years; others are built up very quickly. Let's have a look at a volcano that seemed to appear out of nowhere!

On 20 February 1943, a farmer was working in his cornfield near Paricutín, a remote village in Mexico. All of a sudden, he saw a crack appear in the ground. Hot gas billowed out of it, followed by clouds of ash and broken rock.

16

As the crack widened, streams of lava poured out, burning everything in their path. The farmer and the villagers of Paricutín ran to safety. The eruption buried Paricutín village and a nearby town. All that remained of the buildings was a cathedral spire rising out of the lava.

Paricutín volcano went on erupting for nine years. By this time it stood 410 metres above the cornfield through which it had burst!

Iceland

Surtsey

Look at this island. It's another example of an incredible volcanic birth!

In November 1963, an underwater eruption was recorded off the coast of Iceland. The erupting lava cooled quickly because it came into contact with sea water. Within two days, the island of Surtsey had risen out of the Atlantic Ocean.

18

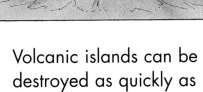

Greece

Thera

Volcanic islands can be destroyed as quickly as they are made.

How can an island be destroyed?

In about 1600 BC, the Greek island of Thera exploded with a series of gigantic blasts. The centre of the island collapsed and was submerged beneath the in-rushing sea. Many people think that Thera is a mythical lost island called Atlantis.

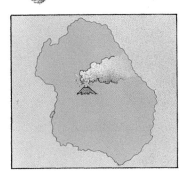

Thera before the eruption

Thera after the eruption

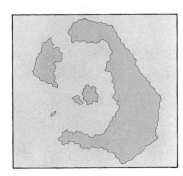

19

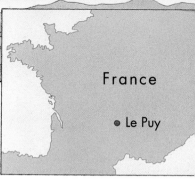

France

● Le Puy

A volcano can be live, dead or **dormant**.

Look at this dead volcano at Le Puy in France. It hasn't erupted for tens of thousands of years. Only the hardened **lava plug** at the centre of the volcano is left. Several hundred years ago, a castle was built on top of it.

20

Is it all right to live on a dead volcano?

Dead volcanoes are not always safe. This is the town of St Pierre in Martinique, which was destroyed when Mont Pelée erupted in 1902. Some 32,000 people died as a result. This volcano was thought to be dead, as it had not erupted for hundreds of years.

Indonesia

Anak Krakatoa

This is Anak Krakatoa in Indonesia. The island rose out of the ashes of the famous Krakatoa, a volcano that was thought to be dormant but which erupted unexpectedly just over 100 years ago.

The volcano on the island of Krakatoa had slept for 200 years. A plug of solid lava blocked its crater. People lived on the island, fished in the seas and didn't worry much about the volcano. But deep inside it pressure was building up.

In August 1883, the island vanished in a series of massive explosions. The third bang was the loudest noise ever recorded on Earth. It was heard in Australia, over 4,000 kilometres away!

Although the explosion killed only a few islanders, the eruption caused gigantic **tsunami waves** that destroyed 163 villages and drowned 36,000 people.

Here is Stromboli, a live volcano off the coast of Italy.

Stromboli has been erupting since ancient times. Explosions take place every fifteen minutes, but this does not stop people visiting and living on the island.

Isn't it dangerous to live near active volcanoes?

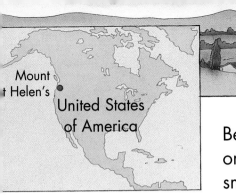

Mount
t Helen's
United States
of America

Because the eruptions
on Stromboli are
small, people believe
it is safe to live there.

All over the world, people continue to live on the
slopes of live volcanoes because
the soil is very fertile.

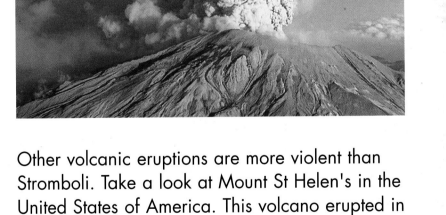

Other volcanic eruptions are more violent than
Stromboli. Take a look at Mount St Helen's in the
United States of America. This volcano erupted in
1980, destroying thousands of square kilometres
of forest in just a few minutes.

Our last stop is Mount Vesuvius in Italy. This is one of the most famous volcanoes of all.

It doesn't look very active!

It looks dormant now, but it has caused terrible destruction in the past. Its most famous eruption, in AD 79, spread a carpet of ash more than six metres deep over the nearby town of Pompeii.

Thousands of people tried to escape by boat or on foot. Nearly everybody who remained was choked to death by ash and poisonous fumes.

Let's go and see what Pompeii looks like today.

When Pompeii was **excavated** during the last century, **archaeologists** were amazed to find that the whole city had been preserved by the volcanic ash.

There were shops, villas, coins, jewellery and even whole **carbonized** eggs and loaves of bread.

You can see the old streets and houses, too!

The people and animals who died had left the shape of their bodies imprinted in the ash. By pouring plaster into these shapes, scientists were able to create accurate models.

Quiz

Now we've reached the end of our volcano adventure. Here is a map of all the volcanoes we've seen. See how many you can name. You can check the maps in the book to see if you've got the right answers.

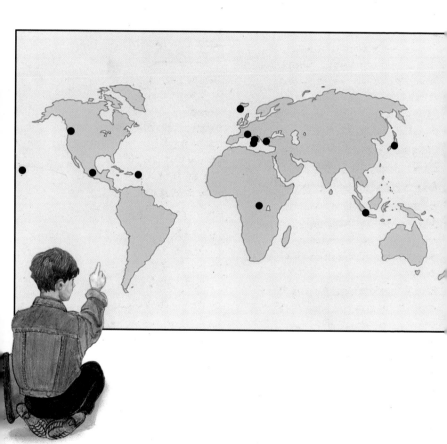

30